STREAMS OF GRACE:

FLOWING THROUGH SPIRIT INSPIRED POETRY

Thomas W. Cahill, Sr.

INTRODUCTION

I am blessed of the Lord to be able to write the words you read in this book of poetry. It is my heavenly Father's gift to me, although I did not recognize it as such in my early years. During those years, my mother, sister, three brothers and myself, lived with our grandparents because our parents had divorced. When my grandfather began having some health problems, my two younger brothers and I, went to live in the Evangelical Children's Home (orphanage} at Lewisburg, PA. I lived there for 4 and a half years. When my mother remarried, I went back to live with her and my step-father.

I was lonely, depressed, and a few times considered suicide. I had no friends because I was very much an introvert. After I had been home about a year, I was drawn by the Holy Spirit to attend a revival service at the Nazarene Church in Johnstown, PA. That night I heard a very clear message on salvation. I went to the altar when the invitation was given. That night I was literally transformed. My old life of sin and loneliness, were exchanged for a "New Life" through the saving blood of the Lord Jesus Christ. When the Scripture says we become a "new creation" in Christ, I can testify to that reality.

I had often talked in rhyme while in the orphanage as a "fun" thing. But after I was saved the rhymes began to take a different form and have a specific message. I wrote my first poem shortly after I was saved in 1956.

I went to college in 1959. Unfortunately I'm not an academically oriented person. I was still very shy and uncertain about things. As part of my assignment in English literature class we were to write something. I wrote a poem but it didn't seem to fit the style needed for the class. This and other circumstances discouraged me from writing poems. At times poetry would simply flow out as I sang or talked, even when preaching or praying. When I could, I'd write it on a scrap paper or napkin.

When I retired in 2008, I began to drive school bus. A few of us became close friends and would joke around during break time. One young lady would often complain about gaining weight, which certainly was not an issue with her. I would write some short poetic comment and give it to her. One day I wrote a little poem about the Lord. She told me I should start writing my poems down. After a lot of encouragement from her and a few others, I wrote my first poem in many years entitled: "A Christmas Poem;" Which I sent as part of our family Christmas card that year. Because I was driving bus, I had an inspiration to write a poem about "bus driving". As my second poem, I wrote, "A Bus Driver's Poem." My boss sent it to the main office and it was published in the company newsletter a few weeks later.

I share all of this, because if it had not been for a determined young lady, Sherry Zimmerman, urging me to write, I probably wouldn't be doing so today. Quite honestly, I have written more poems in the past ten years than in the 40 years prior. It is exciting to finally find a way to share with others the blessings of the Lord through poetry.

I wish to say thank you to so many who have encouraged me to publish my poems over these past few years. I'm grateful to a friend of my wife, Beverly, for putting me in touch with John and Susan Perry who have agreed to publish this book of poems. I am especially thankful to Beverly for her faithful

encouragement, proof reading, and insight,
making this book of poems possible.

Thomas W. Cahill, Sr.

A LITTLE NOTE

A little note from my first night,
In the hospital,
Hope you enjoy:

Good morning Lord
What a night!
Didn't sleep much,
Quite a plight;
Lying in a hospital bed;
Waiting for a snack to be fed.

Just how much sleep I get,
Sure not much, I will bet,
Wake up sir, your blood I must take.
I want to be sure there's no mistake.
Barely did I close my eyes,
When to my great surprise,
Came another to check me out.
Make sure my heart was good and stout.

So now it is this new born day,
The night is gone and I do pray.
I'll get some rest while I can,
Between the tests and the doctor man.

2/1/2022

THE CROSS

The Cross is the place
Where the Savior died
To save you and I
From ruin inside.
He came, that we
Might know the Way
Of love and joy,
And eternal day.
Sin would keep us,
Lost in the dark
But the Cross has done,
It's perfect work,
Of breaking sin's power
That we may live,
Victorious each day
And learn to give,
Jesus the Praise
For delivering our soul,
From the dark side of life,
And make heaven our goal.

T.W. Cahill, Sr.
12/16/ 2011

A CHRISTMAS POEM

A Christmas poem
I write today,
About the One
Who came to pay,
The price for sin
That blights the soul,
So we could live,
Free, pure and whole
Oh what a joy
He brought that night,
To slumbering shepherds
What a sight -
Of angels in the midnight sky
Singing, *"Glory to God on High"*
Away they went,
To seek the King
And share the news
Of the sight they'd seen
So you and I
May join with them
And tell the news
Through voice and pen.

T.W. Cahill, Sr.
12/2011

O WHAT LOVE

O what love could ever compare
With the love of my Lord so dear,
Who in His kind and merciful way,
Lifted me out of the deep miry clay.

O, what love He had for me,
To forgive my sins and set me free,
From the things I had done,
His Name I had cursed; His Way I had shun.

O what love, I can never repay,
For what He has done for me along life's way,
I am a debtor to all mankind,
But most of all, to my Savior sublime.

O What love He has for you,
This great love can fill you too,
If you will open your heart this very hour,
He'll flood your soul with redeeming power.

Then you'll sing His Praises day by day
And enjoy heaven's blessings when you pray.
O what love you will enjoy
Which nothing on earth can destroy.

T.W. Cahill, Sr.
12/17/2011

BEYOND THE HORIZON

Someday beyond the horizon,
We shall meet our Lord and King,
And stand in His Holy Presence,
His Presence to shout and sing.

Someday beyond the horizon,
He shall say to you and I,
Well done good and faithful servant,
You shall never, never die.

Someday beyond the horizon,
Clouds shall gather no more,
Because our Lord and Savior,
Has closed the earthly door.

Someday beyond the horizon,
Darkness shall cease to be,
For the glorious presence of Jesus,
Shall light up eternity.

T.W. Cahill, Sr.
Revised
12/19/2011

ETERNITY WITHOUT THE MASTER

Eternity without the Master,
It shall be a terrible thing,
To feel hell's awful fire,
And torture it will bring.

If you don't know the Master,
Claim Him this very day,
For eternity may come tomorrow
And you will be on your way.

When He calls you unto Him,
Don't turn your head and say,
Not now, Oh Lord, I don't have time,
Maybe some other day.

My friend, this is a mistake too many have
made,
And the Lord has called them home,
They went into Eternity without the Master
Forever, hell's fiery pit they'll roam.

T.W. Cahill, Sr.
8/19/1957

A FRIEND WE NEED

We have a Friend, both you and I
He was hung on a cross for us to die,
He rose again, after three long days,
To return to His old and wonderful ways.

But He stayed on earth, only a little while,
To see it in it's sinful style,
He then ascended to heaven above,
Where He has His everlasting love.

Yes, He is the Friend everyone needs,
No matter how great or small their deeds,
He will help you at any time,
Just pray to Him, the Great and Divine.

T.W. Cahill, Sr.
1958

THE SOUL GOD GAVE ME

What is this thing, they call the soul?
What does it do and where will it go?
That is what so many have asked,
Many a Christian in a daily task.

What do they tell those longing hearts?
"The soul lives on after the body departs".
Where it will go and what it will do,
My dear friend, that's up to you.

Yes, my friend, it's up to you
For you have been given an open view
By the Book which revealed God's way
Throughout the ages - even down to our day.

Truly a Christian in this trying day,
Is assured that his soul is on it's way,
To the home where his Master went to
prepare,
A mansion so bright; beyond earth's care.

But what of you, who are without God?
Whose soul, when it goes, will forever trod,
Hell's fiery pit to never rest,

Because you have neglected God's
righteousness.

T.W. Cahill, Sr.
1/27/1958

LAY SOME SOUL UPON MY HEART

O Blessed Lord I come to Thee,
In humbleness and prayer,
Knowing, Lord, that Thou doest see,
Some soul who needs Thy care.

I seek that Thou, dear Master,
Will lay upon my heart,
This one for whom Thou carest,
That I may help him start,

On his journey upward,
That he may see someday,
Thee in Thy glorious beauty,
And living Thy holy way.

O Master, if Thou art seeking,
Someone to go this day,
To help some lost sinner,
Along life's narrow way,

I, my Lord am willing,
To go out and do for thee,
My very best to win him,
And set the captive free.

O Master, Lord and Savior,
May this the prayer of Christians be,
To go out into this sin-stricken world,
And win those lost souls to Thee,
Amen.

T.W. Cahill, Sr.
3/11/1958

HE LEADETH ME

He leadeth me by His hand,
All the way to glory land,
He hath taken my sins away,
As far as night is from day.

He leadeth me on as each moment does pass,
Though the way is rugged and seems as brass,
He has fulfilled the joy of my soul,
And by this I know heaven is my goal.

He leadeth me to pastures green,
To heights unknown and joys unseen,
He is the One in whom I trust,
He is my Savior: kind, true and just.

He leadeth me now to that golden shore,
Where I shall dwell with Him for ever more.
I love Him so, no words can tell,
All I can say is, O, He's so swell.

T.W. Cahill, Sr.
8/23/1958

I WAIT BEFORE YOU

Lord, I walk before you now,
And in Your Presence, I humbly bow,
Seeking Your grace this very hour,
To keep me strong through Your power.

Lord I need You more than words can say,
I need your help as I walk this way,
Without Your daily cleansing blood,
I'll perish beneath the enemy's flood
Of temptation and pressure to sin.

Only You can cleanse within,
So, my Lord, You are my hope and stay,
The One I need to keep me in the Way,
The joy of life, the freshness of soul,
The One who sustains and makes me whole.

T.W. Cahill, Sr.
December 27, 2011

TODAY

Lord, I sit and rest today,
As I read and as I pray,
For Your grace and guidance sure,
Knowing Your faithfulness will endure
When life is tough and full of pain,
You give us hope and release from strain.

Lord, today I sit, relaxed within
Knowing grace and forgiveness of sin,
Bought through the blood of the Lamb,
The Son of God, the Great I AM.

So this day, as you read these lines,
Look to Jesus for the signs,
Of His grace He gives within,
The peace and hope and freedom from sin.

As you do, this very hour,
You'll discover His grace and mighty power,
Keeping you daily, from sin and shame,
All through the blood and His Holy Name.

T.W. Cahill, Sr.
December 27, 2011

WHEREAS I WAS BLIND

The road was dark and dim the way,
As I wandered blindly from day to day,
Seeking someone who would care,
For a lost sinner in despair.

Then one day my blinded eyes did see,
The way that Christ prepared for me,
He was the One on Whom I cast,
That burden of sin, Oh, at last!

Whereas I was blind now I see,
That rugged road to Calvary
The one, my blessed Savior trod,
To bring lost sinners, like me, to God.

Whereas I was blind, now I see,
The wonderful way Christ prepared for me,
That beautiful home in heaven above,
Where He'll keep me with everlasting love.

T.W. Cahill, Sr.
6/16/1958

O AMERICA WHERE IS OUR GOD

O America, where is our God,
He whose path we once did trod,
We are losing our stand in Him,
All we want are roses in trim.

There shall be no more freedom for us,
Until we turn back to God in trust.
We used to live life filled to the brim,
Now there is barely enough to begin.

O America, we can not go on,
Without trusting faith in our God beyond.
This great country of ours shall surely fall,
If we try to go on without the God of all.

He has prospered us for many years,
And will continue to do so, if we turn back in
tears.
To the God of Glory who will restore our soul
Forgive our sin and make us whole.

Then again His hand we will hold,
As we walk together encouraged and bold,

To take our stand for right and truth,
As we did in the days of our youth.

T.W. Cahill, Sr.
November 11, 1956
Revised January 1, 2012

SOMEWHERE BEYOND THE HORIZON

Somewhere beyond the horizon,
Is the beautiful land of God,
Where someday we'll meet our Savior,
And across the fields we'll trod.

Somewhere beyond the horizon,
We shall walk the streets of gold,
With our long lost loved ones,
As Christ our Lord has foretold.

Somewhere beyond the horizon,
God's promises will be fulfilled,
And we who have lived a Christ like life,
Will be ever, ever thrilled.

T.W. Cahill, Sr.
8/20/1957
Original version

LIFE'S WAY

In seeking to be strong, we must become
weak,
That the glory of life may be His each day,
That the strength we have be not our own,
But rather be that which comes from His
Throne.

In weariness and drain come life's long days,
But grace and strength are always His ways.
His Promise is true in each lonely hour,
He gives you strength and heavens power.

So filled with pain, within, without,
There seems no way to conquer doubt,
Look up, look long, you soon will see,
The Light of day and your destiny.

In that moment life will be renewed,
You'll know His Hand is guiding you,
Through all your doubt, struggle and pain
You'll rejoice each day free from life's strain.

T.W. Cahill, Sr.
2007/1/21
Revised
1/4/2012

RISE UP O MY SOUL

Rise up o my soul, do not despair,
In your God, there's love and care.
Do not fear in these dark days,
Rise up my soul; give God praise.

Rise up O my soul, rejoice in God,
For someday His golden streets you'll trod,
Because He lifted you from the deep miry clay,
And set your feet on the Rock to stay.

Again, I say rise up my soul,
Rise up and make God's kingdom your goal.
Fight your battles day by day,
Don't fret over sorrows along the way.

For all the clouds in a moment are past,
If upon Christ Jesus our burdens we cast.
The sun will break through with glorious
throng,
So rise up O my soul; praise God in song.

T.W. Cahill, Sr.
2/9/1958
Original words

LIVING WATER

In my soul is a well of living water,
Springing up within me, Glory be to the
Father,
For He has filled me with the Blessed Holy
Ghost,
And I'm so happy now that of my God I boast.

He is ever loving, ever kind and true,
He thrills my very life in everything I do,
And puts within my heart a peace beyond
compare,
That I, with many others, wish to share.

O how my heart is rejoicing,
Of the love that God is voicing
Within my soul day and night
To keep me from wrong and guide me in the
right.

T.W. Cahill, Sr.
1958
Original words

WHY DO YOU SORROW O MY SOUL

Why do you sorrow O my soul,
Is not heaven your only goal?
Do not fret over things that pain
Through this earth with all it's strain.

Why do you sorrow, O child of God,
While along life's road you daily trod.
Did not He from His Throne above,
Lift you up through His great love?
From sin and sorrow one glorious day
To set your feet on the Rock to stay.

Why do you sorrow on this earth's waste,
When God's blessings you can taste,
Through the Blood of the Lord Jesus Christ,
Who on Calvary's cross has paid,
The price for sins that you had done
And by His death the Victory won.

Why do you sorrow over the little things,
That this earth, with its trouble brings.
Why not look to the everlasting God
And hear Him say with a smiling nod,
Fear not, my child for I am near,

To wipe away every tear.
I, your God, will never leave
You in the sorrow ever to grieve.

T.W. Cahill, Sr.
2/9/1958
Rewritten
1/16/2018

PLEASE, DEAR FRIEND

Please, dear friend, I ask of you,
Search your heart the whole way through,
And if you find the slightest thing,
That to your life destruction would bring,
Yield it to your Lord just now
As before Him you humbly bow.

I pray that He will kindly show,
To you, each and every foe.
O, please dear friend, this very day,
Give your heart to His Holy way
That walking in His righteousness
He, your life can surely bless

May, my friend, our God above
Pour out on you His Beauty and Love,
And show to you what He can do,
When we keep ourselves holy and true
By reading His Word every day
Seeking His Presence as we pray.

May there be no flaw in you,
As He guides, your whole life through,
May He keep you on the narrow road,
And guide you safely to your heavenly abode

Where someday you'll be with Him
Free from sorrow, free from sin.

T.W. Cahill, Sr.
2/2/1958
Rewritten
1/16/2018

BLESSED SPRING

When the buds come out on the plants and
trees,
And you hear the humming and buzzing of
bees,
You know it is that time of the year,
O yes, our blessed spring is here!

When the grass awakes from its long winter's
sleep,
And the roaring of the brook sounds so deep,
You see the beauty that God did bring,
When He opened the season of blessed spring.

The trees on the hillside bloom so fair,
And the flowers around them their beauty
share,
They all look forward to a beautiful thing,
It's what we call, our blessed spring.

The sun is in the cloudless sky,
And you hear the birds sing as they are flying
by,
This is the beauty

that God does bring
To show us His love of a blessed spring.

T.W. Cahill, Sr.
1957, spring, Original words

JESUS, MY FRIEND

O Jesus my Friend and my Lord,
I lean upon Your Holy Word,
When all around my soul gives way,
You are my only hope and stay.

When the tempests toss and billows roll,
You are the strength of my soul,
In the hour when my plans fail,
Your grace, O Lord will still prevail.

My Jesus I need You, my heart is sore,
Life seems so vain and very poor,
There is no end to my agony,
Life is nothing that I can see.
The pouring rain, the gathering cloud,
Hardly seem to make life worthwhile.

T.W. Cahill, Sr.
8/19/1975

Written during a very difficult time in my life.
Revised 1/4/2012

THIS JOURNEY I TAKE

This journey I take from day to day,
Singing my song along life's way,
Of Jesus my Lord who faithfully leads,
Through storms, and pain, and delightful
deeds.

Surely He is the Faithful One,
Who urges us to walk till life is done
In holiness and righteousness,
In all we do,

That in the end He may say,
Come home my child,
Your journey's through,
Now live with me, forever new.

T.W. Cahill, Sr.
3/30/2013

IN QUIETNESS

In quietness and stillness
I sit in the rain
Listening carefully to
Life's chaos and strain
For the voice of the Master
To drift through the air
And lift from my heart
Life's burdens and care

Looking carefully; expectantly
Up toward to the sky
For there shall I see
His grace by and by
He knows my need
So I quietly wait
In the dew and the rain
For His Glory so great.

T.W. Cahill, Sr.
5/6/1988

HIS GUIDING HAND

The Lord will lead us by His Guiding Hand
Through all the struggles and fears of this
earthen land,
The Devil will tempt us along the way,
But His Guiding Hand is there to stay.

Though we are troubled and in despair,
His Guiding Hand is always there,
When we are sick and close to death,
He guides us through, to our last breath.

When we close our eyes, to life on earth,
And have joyfully received the *"second birth"*,
He will guide us through the air,
To the land of joy, a land so fair.
Yes, He is guiding us by His Hand,
To that glorious and righteous land.

T.W. Cahill, Sr.
1957
Revised
12/17/2011

HERE I SIT

Here I sit along the road
A happy frog, a lonely toad

So I go along life's way
Wondering what I should say

No one to talk with me
As I sit under the elephant tree

Rambling words seem to come
Here and there and then some

Where I go no one would know
How to follow or what to show

But then it's good for you to see
The wonder of the elephant tree

So what you say would only be
The wonder of little old me.

T.W. Cahill, Sr.
12/27/2012

CHRISTMAS TIME

Christmas time is a happy time
When life is full of song and rhyme
So Merry Christmas to all who read
These lines now written with lightening speed.

Yes we write our song of joy and peace
The birth of Christ brings sweet release
From the fear and pain some days can bring
But peace on earth is the song we sing.

Be blest this day as we celebrate
The birth of Christ on this special date
Come join our song as we sing just now
And in His Presence humbly bow.

T.W. Cahill, Sr.
12/24/2014

REJOICE IN THE HOLY ONE

Let the rocks keep silent
As we lift our voice in Praise
Lifting up our hosannas before the Throne
Delighting in the Holy One
Who Redeemed for His own.

Sing above the storms of life
When waves so fiercely roll
Rejoicing in the Mighty One
Who cleansed and made you whole.

Rise upon the wings of Praise
Into the bright blue sky
Knowing for certain
That your Victory is nigh.

T.W. Cahill, Sr.
Date unknown

THE RISING SUN

Up from the east
Comes the rising sun
With radiant beams
Of morning light
Breaking the darkness
Of the night.

The red sky shining
In the morning dawn
Makes me think
Of the World beyond,
Of it's Glorious beauty
We can't see,
Until we reach eternity.

This winter scene is
Quite a view
Of the Majestic Art
And Beauty too
That only God
Can bring to be
Such a blessing
For you and me.

T.W. Cahill, Sr.
1/4/2017
Revised 1/26/2022

COME HOLY SPIRIT

Come Holy Spirit
Indwell my soul,
Restoring, cleansing;
Making me whole,
Filled with Your Presence,
Through and through,
Blessed with Your Glory,
Your Holiness too.

Full of Your praise,
Your joy, Your grace
Sanctified fully
In Your Resting Place,
Where You alone
Dwell deep within,
Keeping; cleansing
From all sin.

Your Power and Beauty
Flood my soul,
Your Perfect redemption
Makes me whole,
I will praise You forever
For filling me now,

With Your Glory and Grace,
And Your Cleansing Power.

T.W. Cahill, Sr.
08/09/2015

A CHRISTMAS POEM I WRITE

A Christmas poem I write tonight,
Sitting in my chair,
Waiting quietly for the time,
When I shall kneel in prayer,
To praise His Name for coming down,
From Heaven's Throne on high,
To live a life of poverty,
And then for me, to die.

Tis Christmas time once again,
When we reflect on Him,
And talk about His coming here,
To set us free from sin,
Yet why do we so often live,
As if He died in vain.

Let us live by His Grace,
A life that honors Him,
And daily walk by His Power,
Above all strife and sin,
That men may see His Holiness,
In all we say and do,
And know the Christ of Christmas,
Is real through me and you.

T.W. Cahill, Sr.
12/24/2015

YES, MY LORD

Yes, my Lord,
I bow this day,
Before Thy Holy Throne,
My heart does say,
To Thee, Oh Lord,
I am Thine alone.
Truly, Lord,
You are mine,
Your Glory, Love
And Grace Divine.
I cherish deeply,
In my soul,
For You, my Savior,
Have made me whole.

T.W. Cahill, Sr.
12/22/2016

A NEW DAY

A new day is before me
The past is left behind
The joy of what it was
Is blessed and sublime.

A new day lies before me,
Where it leads I do not know,
I follow close beside Him,
Wherever He may go.

A new day lies before me,
I journey on by faith,
A new day I am offered,
With Him, I know it's safe.

A new day lies before me,
Some friends have passed me by,
But new ones He will give me,
As we journey side by side.

A New Life lies before me,
All fresh and clean from Him,
Whose Blood has thoroughly washed,
And purified from sin.

A New Life lies before me,
With someone I do not know
Whose loving heart is open,
To the way that we should go.

Yes, we shall meet together,
And onward from that day,
Serve the King of Glory,
To praise Him and to pray.

A new life now we have,
As we walk along,
Serving Christ our Saviour,
In gladness and in song.

A new life lies before us,
What joy and grace He gives,
Together we would serve Him,
And in His presence live.

T.W. Cahill, Sr.
3/11/2017

A NEW YEAR HAS DAWNED

A New Year has dawned
A new time to see
What the Lord has planned
Just for you and me.

It is quite exciting,
As we should know,
His Holy Presence with us
As onward we would go.

This Truth we have from His Word,
No harm will come our way
For He has promised to keep,
And lead us day by day

Though storms and conflicts
Will surely come
Throughout the year ahead
Victory He will give
Over every single one.

T.W. Cahill, Sr.
1/1/2016

A QUIET PLACE

Here I am,
In a quiet place,
Waiting Lord,
To see Your Face,
Your Smile of Love,
I would see,
As I wait on bended knee.

Here I am,
In this quiet place,
Resting Lord upon Your Grace,
Looking always to be with Thee
That Your Glory I may see
Shining forth upon each day,
As I journey on my way.

T.W. Cahill, Sr.
12/27/2016

ALONE I STAND

Alone I stand
No one to listen
No one to care
Life is empty
I'm in despair...

My friends are gone
No one to stand and pray
As I sit and stay
In my tears
Alone today.

Why Lord are others so blest
Why is my life such a mess
What have I done to stand alone
When others have family and a home.

Your blessing I need so much this night
Let me see Your power Your might
Ease the pain lift the load
Weighing heavy on my soul
Please Lord make me whole.

T.W. Cahill, Sr.
9/20/2014

PERFECT PEACE

Amen!
Oh the gladness of His Spiritual Blessings.
They fill my soul today.
Oh the wonder of His goodness that leads me
all the way.
Through every storm and trial of life
His Glory leads and stills the strife
Keeping my soul in perfect peace.

T.W. Cahill, Sr.
3/14/2017

BE PREPARED

Be prepared to live or die,
Never worry, never sigh.
With Christ as Saviour,
Lord and King
Your spirit will forever sing.

Praises from a heart made pure
Prepared to live forevermore
So death is just a stepping stone
That brings me to His Holy Throne
Where I can bow on bended knee
And praise His Name eternally.

T.W. Cahill, Sr.
3/31/2017

BE STRONG AND OF GOOD COURAGE

Be strong and of good courage
Our Master says tonight
The battle is not yours
Tis His to win the fight.

Be strong and of good courage
Stand still before His Throne
The victory is yours
Through Him and Him alone.

Be strong and of good courage
Hear His Word to you
I AM your Lord
I will see you through.

Be strong and of good courage
Rest quietly in Me
The powers of hell are crushed
Beneath the cursed tree.

Be strong and of good courage
For I have overcome
Every foe you face
And the victory won.

T.W. Cahill, Sr.
4/16/2017

IN THE QUIET OF THE MORNING HOURS

In the quiet of the morning hours
I will rise and pray
Listen to what my Master said
As He leads me through my day.

Surely in this quiet place
All strain and struggle gone
My soul shall be renewed
Filled with joy and song.

How wonderful this quiet place of prayer
Prepares me for another day
His love and joy to share
With those who need hope and peace
To lift them from despair.

So thank You Lord for my quiet place
That blesses this soul of mine
Fills me with Your Holiness
As at Your table I dine.

T.W. Cahill, Sr.
1/14/2022

AN INVITATION

Come you who are weary and worn
To My rest for your soul
Cease from your laboring efforts
And I will make you whole.

Come you who are thirsty
For something to satisfy
Your dry, barren spirit
Come to My well of endless supply.

Come you who are hungering
For that which would give
Life to your dead empty spirit
That you might truly live

Feed at My banquet table
Your soul to satisfy
And you will eternally live.
My Name to glorify.

T.W. Cahill, Sr.
1/26/2022

PRAYING FATHERS

This day we rejoice
In the goodness of our God
In the grace He has given us
As this road we have trod.

For our fathers who showed
His kind gentle way
By living a righteous life
But not much did they say.

Reading the Word
Of God each night
As the family would gather 'round
Listening with a quiet heart
Not uttering a single sound

Then bowing his head did pray
For wife and every child
You could feel his yearning heart
Was humble, meek and mild.

Dear Lord please give us
fathers,
Like these men of old
Whose lives were richer
Than the purest of gold.

Give us men of the Word
Who know how to pray
Touching the gates of heaven
Each and every day,

Lifting their family upward
Before Thy Holy Throne.
Calling each one by name
Who are his very own.

From a heart of love
With yearnings deep and strong
Praying that he will see them
Someday in heaven above.

T.W. Cahill, Sr.
1/26/2022

ANOTHER BEAUTIFUL DAY

It's another beautiful day
The Father of Glory
Has sent our way
To honor and praise Him
For all that He's done
Giving us redemption,
Life in His Son.

So let's lift our voices
And joyfully sing
Songs of glad tidings
And let them wing
Their way up to heaven
Before His Holy Throne
Praise from our hearts
That are His very own.

T.W. Cahill, Sr.
6/26/2017

AS A MIGHTY RIVER

As a mighty river
Flows the love of God
By His Spirit glorious
From the Throne above.

Sweeping ever onward
Through both time and space
Moving every object
Into the proper place.

Washing away all bitterness
Selfishness and shame
Bringing in its wake
A transformed life and name.

Yes this mighty river
Flows forever on
Healing, lifting broken lives
And giving them a song.

T. W. Cahill, Sr.
1/15/2016

THE PROMISE

At the close of the day
When news is bad and hearts are sore
There is the promise from the world beyond
My peace I give with assurance
That if you will endure
My purpose will be accomplished with
certainty
And you shall see without question
That there is absolute victory.

T.W. Cahill, Sr.
4/1/2020

BE STRONG MY FRIEND

Be strong my friend
'Tis ever true
The Lord of Glory
Cares for you.

When the battle is tough
And all hell breaks loose
The Power of God
Will make a noose

To wrap around
The devil's crew
So they are powerless
To do harm to you.

All you hear
Is a roaring sound
But harm can't come
For Satan's bound.

So victory is yours
You can be sure
Through Christ alone
You shall endure.

T.W. Cahill, Sr.
4/15/2017

A BEAUTIFUL DAY

A beautiful day, yet sad it is
Pondering the events of long ago
Remembering how the Son of God
Was beaten and scorned by His very own
Who hated Him for the things He had done.

Yet we today, sad but true
Sometimes those very things we do
By the lives we live and yet profess
That we are His but don't possess
The transforming grace of righteousness.

Instead we live as before
No change has come and we ignore
The Cross where He died this very day
To remove our sins far away
And cleanse us daily through His Blood
That we be pure and clean within
And no longer walk in sin.

That those around would surely know
The Cross was the final blow
To sin and hell in the human heart
And God had finally done His part,

To restore our soul to victory
Through Christ who died upon the tree
And won the battle against all sin
That we might live each day within
A life of joy and righteousness
That all may see His Holiness.

T.W. Cahill, Sr.
4/14/2017

BEFORE THE THRONE OF GOD I BOW

Before the Throne of God I bow,
Seeking for His Holiness,
Longing for the glory of His love,
Radiant joy and righteousness.

Within myself I am sin,
Riddled through and through,
But hallelujah through His Blood
I am created new.

Hear my voice oh Lord above,
As I bow this day,
Flood my soul in purity
And lead me in Thy way.

T.W. Cahill Sr.
12/9/2020

BLESSED BE THE LORD OF GLORY

Blessed be the Lord of Glory,
I will ever tell the story,
Of HIS MIGHTY grace and power,
That keeps my soul by the hour,
In joy and victory,
love and peace,
Delighting always in blessed ease,
Because He keeps me strong and well,
In the conflict with sin and hell,
His Blood repels the demon force,
His Spirit drives them far off course,
They can not touch this soul of mine,
He Keeps, protects by His power sublime.

T.W. Cahill, Sr.
8/7/2013

BLESS THE LORD O MY SOUL

Bless the Lord oh my soul,
Bless His Holy Name.
To Him we sing our songs,
Of redeeming love that came
Lifting us up from sin and sorrow
Giving us hope for a new tomorrow.

From His riches we have received
The fullness of blessing
He freely gives
To all who will serve Him
And in His presence live.

Why not join in the journey,
As many have gladly done,
And live each day for Jesus
The Holy, Glorious One.

Who forever lives in glory
Where we shall be someday,
Enjoying all the blessings
He has in store

For those who follow
Close by His side every day.

T. W. Cahill, Sr.
12/10/2021

CAN I THIS HOUR?

Can I this hour humbly say
Christ my Lord leads the way
Through thick and thin I trust Him now
In victory, joy and hope I bow
Knowing He'll keep me safe, secure
With Him I know I'll endure
All that comes to me in life
Whether peace or joy, sorrow or strife.

Above them all He lifts me up
That in His presence I may sup
Full of gladness, freedom from sin
As His Spirit purifies within
Filling my heart with heavenly love
Flowing freely from His Throne above
To bless and lift those lost in pain
That they may rise and hope again.

T.W. Cahill, Sr.
12/22/2021

COME

Come you who are weary and worn
To My rest for your soul
Cease from your laboring efforts
And I will make you whole.

Come you who are thirsty
For something to satisfy
Your dry, barren spirit
Come to My well of endless supply.

Come you who are hungering
For that which would give
Life to your dead empty spirit
Feed at My banquet table
And you will eternally live.

T.W. Cahill, Sr.
6/26/2017

CHRISTMAS CARD POEM

Look closely at what you see,
Behold the miracle of Majesty.
The Lamb of God, it was a must,
To save the world from sin's dark night
He sent the Star of Heavenly Light.

Look closely at what you see
The Lion of Judah, it must be,
The King of Glorious Royalty,
Whose power and strength will destroy,
All sin, rebellion and evil ploy.
Yet, gentle eyes, for all who seek,
The Prince of Peace, humble and meek.

Look so closely and you will see,
The light of life for you and me,
Nestled quietly in a manger bed,
His glorious light on us to shed,
The hope of life, instead of death,
Made possible by His final breath.
He rose again, this Lion, Lamb,
King of Glory, the Great I AM.

Look closely at the crowd, gathered round,
From every nation they are found,
Rich and poor, shepherd, king,
All have come to humbly bring,

Their gifts of honor, joy and praise,
To the Babe of Bethlehem,
Their songs they raise.

T.W. Cahill, Sr.
12/23/2016

A FATHER'S DAY POEM

This day we rejoice
In the Goodness of God
In the Grace He has given us
As this road we have trod.

For our fathers who showed
His kind gentle way
By living the life,
Not much did they say.

Reading the Word
As the family sat around,
Bowing his head he prayed
For his wife and each child
You could feel his heart
Was humble and mild.

Dear Lord give us fathers
Like these men of old
Whose life we respect
They were richer than gold

Give us men of the Word
Who know how to pray.
And how to touch heaven
Every day
Lifting their family

Before the Throne
Naming each one

From a heart full of love
Praying that he'll see all
In heaven above.

T.W. Cahill, Sr.
6/18/2017

'TIS AMAZING GRACE

Amazing grace how sweet the sound
That saved a wretch like me
Lifted me up from the miry clay
Setting my spirit free.

What love it was that sought me out
When I a rebel was
A love beyond all human thought
This blessed redeeming fount,
That flowed like sweet perfume
Touching my tired, weary heart
To heal its sin cursed wound.

O what amazing grace that touched my broken
soul
Bringing hope and love to fill it's empty hole
What can I say of heaven's love
it reaches so far beyond
Our wildest dreams and the evening sun.

T.W. Cahill, Sr.
1/21/2022

COME O COME

Come O come Lord of Glory
Fill our hearts afresh, anew
With Your sanctifying beauty
Cleanse us Lord through and through.

May we know without a question
All Your majesty and love
Purifying every corner
Holy Spirit, heavenly dove.

T. W. Cahill, Sr.
1/16/2019

COME O HOLY SPIRIT

Come O Holy Spirit
Upon this heart of mine,
Fill it fresh and new
With purifying fire
Cleansing from all sin
Through the blood of Calvary

Come O Holy Spirit
Abide within my soul
That my heart would honor You
As the ages roll.

Come O Holy Spirit
And cause my heart to sing
With joy and with gladness
The glories of my King

Come O Holy Spirit
Set my heart aflame
With the beauty of His holy love
In Jesus matchless name.

Come O Holy Spirit
Live within my heart
Purify from selfishness
And holy love impart.

May I live each day
For the glory of His Name
That those who walk beside me
Will never be the same.

T.W. Cahill, Sr.
8/8/2017

DAY OF TRIUMPH

Early in the morning they did rise
Three broken hearted women
With tears in their eyes
Slowly they made their way
Toward the garden tomb.
In those early morning hours
Of sadness, sorrow and gloom.

Who shall roll away
The mighty stone they said
Never thinking that Christ the Lord
Had risen from the dead,
With wonder and amazement
They stared in shocked surprise
The stone was rolled away
From death He did arise
Triumphant over death, hell and the grave
That a lost world He could save.

In fear, joy and wonder
These faithful women three
Ran to tell the others
The miracle they did see
The tomb of Christ was empty
And angels had declared

That He'd meet them in Galilee
As He with them had shared.

T.W. Cahill, Sr.
4/12/2020

CONSUMED BY HIS GLORY

Consumed by His glory deep within
My soul echoes His glorious praise,
Compelled by His Spirit of holy love
My heart sings with life from heaven above.

Beyond all description this marvelous Grace
Flows through my soul
Without a trace
Not of my own doing
Could the majesty come,
But only through God the Son.

Consumed I say by love divine
Filled with His Spirit
What joy sublime
Keeping me daily in this world of woe
Cleansing, sustaining as onward I go.

T.W. Cahill, Sr.
11/13/2021

LORD OF GLORY

Dear Lord of Glory
Come to our aid
Our nation is broken
Our hearts are very sad
We need Your presence
And power this day
Before our worship
Becomes as they say
Illegal and rejected
By those who hate
Your beauty and redemption
Because You take
Broken, shattered lives
And by transforming grace
Change the world around us
Into a much better place.

T.W. Cahill, Sr.
7/17/2020

DEEP FLOWING RIVER

Oh that deep flowing river
That never shall run dry
Supplies the grace we need.
Until the day we die.

Oh that deep flowing river
That flows so deep within
Cleansing, keeping our hearts each day
Purifying from all sin.

Oh that deep flowing river.
That nourishes the soul
Nurturing and blessing
Making fully whole.

T.W. Cahill, Sr.
3/27/2017

CAME FORTH

Early in the morning
Before the sun could rise
The Mighty, Victorious Christ
Came forth
From among the dead.
In radiant beauty He shown,
He broke the morning dawn
Redeeming grace to offer all
And set them free from sin.

T.W. Cahill, Sr.
Easter 2021

EASTER JOY

On this Glorious Easter morning,
Christ from the grave was torn
Up He arose from the sting of death
To give new life and eternal breath
To all who bow at His feet
Forsaking sin and defeat
When they rise with life anew
With His glory in plain view
Walking each day in His Righteousness
Knowing perfect love and holiness.

T. W. Cahill, Sr.
4/3/2021

FATHER OF GRACE AND GLORY

Father of grace and glory.
I bow before Your Throne,
With praise and adoration,
For You and You alone.

Your gracious love and mercy,
You give to me this day
Undeserving as I am
You give and don't delay.

How kind and gentle your Presence
Your sweetness and Your love,
That fills my heart with gladness,
And mercy from heaven above.

T.W. Cahill, Sr.
4/13/2017

FILL ME WITH YOUR PERFECT LOVE

Fill me with Your perfect love
Lord of grace divine
Penetrate every part
My soul, my heart, my mind.

Let every movement, every thought
Be filled with perfect love
Until my soul is raptured
To heaven up above.

But until then my Lord I pray
Let me live for Thee
That those around may feel Your love
And Your glory see.

Then seeking you as their Lord
And Saviour from their sin
Repenting of their acts of wrong
Becoming born again.

May live a life that honors You
Every single day
In all they say and do

Let my life demonstrate
Your power and holiness

Until they long dear Lord
For All Your righteousness.

T.W. Cahill, Sr.
Date unknown

FLY HIGH EAGLE FLY HIGH

Fly high eagle fly high
Up, up into the sky
Above the storm
Wind and rain
Fly high fly into the sky.

Fly high eagle fly high
Above the mountain
Crags and rocks
Fly high eagle fly high
Free from all bondage
Never in a box.

T.W. Cahill, Sr.
8/25/2021

GIVE ME A FAITH

Give me a faith
That will not shrink
Amidst the storms of life
A faith dear Lord
That will not bend
In struggles and in strife
When conflicts come
And hell breaks loose
Upon my weary soul
May I stand with head held high
And trust dear Lord in You
Knowing that Your faithfulness
Will see me safely through.

T.W. Cahill, Sr.
5/27/2017

HAPPY RESURRECTION DAY!

Happy Resurrection Day!
Amen and Amen.
I serve a Risen Savior
Who sits upon His Throne
Living, gloriously living,
Calling me His own
Filling each day with victory
Over sin and shame and hell
Oh yes, He is Risen
This I'll ever tell
To all of those who ask me
If I know for sure
That Jesus Christ is Risen
Yes, He's Risen
And lives forevermore.

T.W. Cahill, Sr.
4/5/15

HERE I SIT IN CANDLE LIGHT

Here I sit in candle light
Waiting for the unfolding night
Wondering what will come my way
As I bow my head and pray.

There is nothing for me to do,
But rest my weary heart in You,
As life moves along in uneventful ways,
Changing with the winds of time every hour of
every day.

T.W. Cahill, Sr.
12/9/19

HIS ABIDING PEACE

His abiding peace fills my soul
His purifying Spirit makes me whole
His blood that cleanses from all sin
Gives victory each day as I walk in Him.

Rejoicing love fills my heart
From His presence I won't depart
For power and grace He gives to me
The Holy Spirit and victory.

Bless His name who sits on the Throne
For redeeming me as His own
Nothing this life offers this day
Could ever turn me from the Narrow Way.

T.W. Cahill, Sr.
4/14/20

A BIRTHDAY POEM

A birthday poem
For a special friend
Who blesses those she knows
And brings a smile to everyone wherever she
may go.

Hoping that your day went well
And had a joyful end
With those who love and care for you
Great moments you did spend

Who blesses your life every day,
With gladness joy and peace
A happy, happy birthday for you my friend I
pray.
Your blessings to increase.

T.W. Cahill, Sr.
3/5/17

HIS NAME IS JESUS

His Name is Jesus
King of Kings
His home is Glory
Where the redeemed sing
Songs of praise with voices strong
Every moment all day long.

This Jesus is coming
In Almighty Power
Knees will bend
In that glad hour.
Reviving the weary
Saint of God
Who has been pleading
The power of redeeming blood
For their broken,
Sin cursed world
Pleading for darkness
To be quickly hurled
Into the pit from which it came
Through the power of Jesus Name.

Rebel hearts will yield and pray,
Seeking forgiveness in that day.
The Lord of Glory shall
Change the heart
Of those who repent and turn from sin

Cleansing, forgiving, transforming within.
Riots will cease and chaos stop
For the Lord of Glory has changed the heart
Of all who bow before His Throne
Who now He claims as His own.

These will change the world around
Righting wrong and bringing sound
Peace and blessings to everyone
No matter what they may have done
Restoring hope to this shattered world
Their banner of grace and kindness unfurled.

T.W. Cahill, Sr.
6/27/20

HAPPY RESURRECTION DAY

Happy Resurrection Day
To all my friends out there
This day we celebrate
God's power and His care,

For had this day never come
We would still be lost
It is the glory of our Christ
The victory of the Cross

Because He arose from the grave
In Mighty Victory
We, once dead in sin's dark night
Are from sin set free.

T.W. Cahill, Sr.
4/16/17

HE IS AMAZING

He is amazing
This marvelous King of Kings
Lord of Lords, Prince of Peace
The Mighty God is He.

To walk with Him
From day to day
Is awesome
I do know
For He keeps me safe
Wherever I should go.

If you serve Him
With a humble heart
You will surely say
He is faithful in all He does
He keeps me in the Way.

T.W. Cahill, Sr.
Date unknown

ANYTHING TO EAT

Have you anything to eat my child
Jesus said one day to me
Standing on the shore of life
Clearly I could not see
Who called my name with deep concern
That I should nourished be

As I rowed my empty boat,
More closely to the shore
My heart began to burn within
For something more and more.

Then I knew who called my name
And longed to feed my soul
'twas Jesus Christ Lord of life
Who longed to make me whole.

I'd struggled through the night
To try to satisfy,
My lonely aching heart
From which He heard my cry

He had come to meet me there
On the shore of life
And fill me with His tranquil peace
Instead of sin and strife.

His gentle voice in the morning air
Was so sweet and rich to me
This loving Christ had come that day
That I might nourished be.

T.W. Cahill, Sr.
Revised T.W. Cahill, Sr.

2/4/22

BESIDE THE FIRE

Here I sit beside the fire
Waiting for my heart's desire
Of His mighty grace and power
To keep my soul every hour
In His love beyond compare
Joyfully walking in The Way
Of Christ my Savior every day.

T.W. Cahill, Sr.
1/15/16

I AGREE, AND STAND WITH YOU

I agree, and stand with you
upon the promise,
faithful and true.
It is our rock
In a weary land,
Our water of life,
In desert sand.
Our joy and hope,
When all else fails,
His promise holds,
And will prevail.
No power of hell,
Can shake the soul,
That rests on Jesus,
To keep them whole.

T.W. Cahill, Sr.
8/2/13

I AM UPHELD

I am upheld
by His Almighty Hand,
No power of hell,
no threat of man,
Can cause me to fear,
come what may,
His glory, His grace
will lead the way.

So no power on earth,
Nor none below,
Can triumph over those,
Who are held in His hand.
Who trust in His faithfulness,
As they journey along,
Joyfully singing their victory song.

T.W. Cahill, Sr.
7/14/14

I BOW BEFORE MY FATHER

I bow before my Father
And lift you up in prayer
The burden you now carry
Is grief beyond compare.

In the darkness of this hour
May His Light you see
And sense His Holy presence
Through the Cross of Calvary

May His Peace beyond all measure
Fill your hearts and life
And the beauty of His love
Keep you through this night.

Knowing that the morning
Will come for you some day
And those you miss so much
You'll meet along the way.

T.W. Cahill, Sr.
5/7/17

BEFORE THE THRONE OF GLORY

I bow before the Throne of Glory,
Rejoicing in His grace
That floods my soul so fully,
As I look upon His face.

No one can grasp the wonder,
Of this Majestic King,
Until they sit before Him,
And hear the angels sing.

Glory to the Holy One,
Who sits upon the Throne,
He redeems the lost from sin,
And calls them His very own.

So join me here at this place,
Where devils fear to tread,
And sing the songs of victory,
We are no longer dead,

But alive and vibrant,
Day by day, free from hell's dark night,
Living daily by His grace,
In purified delight.

T.W. Cahill, Sr.
8/3/13

BEFORE YOUR THRONE

I bow before Your Throne
Oh Lord of love and grace
I seek Your Holy will
The smile upon Your Face.

I bow before Your Throne
This another day
Longing for Your glory
To lead me all the way.

I bow before Your Throne
Oh Holy Lord of love
Looking for Your guidance
That comes from heaven above.

I bow before Your Throne
Father of life and truth
Knowing that You will keep me
As Your transforming proof

That You have total power
To break the bonds of sin
And purify the heart
Through the Blood that flows within.

Tom Cahill, Sr.
1/17/17

I DWELL ON THE MIDST

I dwell on the midst
Of the praise of My people
Where hearts are rejoicing
In My faithfulness and Love

Where souls are renewed
With the strength of My WORD
The grandest story
Man ever heard

There where praise
Rules the heart
Where joy unspeakable
Is always a part

Of life at it's fullest
And grandest theme
Miracles abound,
Love is supreme.

So praise My Name
Lift up your song
I dwell in your midst
It won't be long

Til victory comes
To those who sing
Who praise My Name
In everything.

T.W. Cahill, Sr.
5/12/17

I GATHERED IN FOR PRAYER

I gathered in for prayer this morning
Before my Father's Throne,
With all the Family, He purchased for His
own,
Through the precious blood of Jesus, upon
that rugged tree,
Where He died to break sin's power
And set us captives free.

I gathered in for prayer this morning
Before my Father's Throne,
Hungering for His Holiness, to permeate my
soul,
That through this day I might live
A life pure and whole,
That some poor broken, shattered life,
Might be delivered from conflict and strife.

I gathered in for prayer this morning
Before my Father's Throne,
Interceding for those still lost,
That they might hear His Word
And know the price it cost,

To set them free from sin's dark night,
And bring them to the place
Of His redeeming light.

T.W. Cahill, Sr.
10/31/21

GOD THE MIGHTY HOLY GHOST

Is moving across this weary land
With hope and Joy for all
Who heed His command
To forsake all sin and all ungodly ways
Turn their heart heavenward and the Name of
Jesus Praise.

Seek Him who died for you
And open up your soul
He will come in loving Grace
Transform and make you whole.

This nation now before Him stands In
judgement and in sin
But if we who call upon his name
Will humbly enter in
To walk with Him the Holy One
Who sits upon the Throne
And by the Holy Spirit
Honor the Father and the Son
This nation will be spared
And the Victory won.

T.W. Cahill Sr
1/25/22

I STAND AMAZED AT HIS GLORY

Every single day
How He leads and guides us
Along life's narrow way.

Giving us His Wisdom,
Kindness, love and grace
Showing forth His Majesty
In every single place.

Granting me the privilege
Of meeting one like you
Is such a awesome honor
It thrills me through and through.

What a Wonderful Saviour
Who blesses day by day
And leads us both together
In His Holy Way.

So my friend I'm grateful
For His Love and Grace
That keeps us close together
Beneath His Smiling Face.

T.W. Cahill Sr
1/17/17

IF IT WASN'T FOR THE LIGHTHOUSE

That sits upon the shore
My broken shattered life
Would certainly be no more.

The night was dark and dreary
The winds were raging on
My ship was at the mercy
Of a fierce and deadly storm.

Then off across the waters
I saw a light so dim
It shined through the darkness
Of brokenness and sin.

With hope I turned toward it
So glad was I to see
The Light of life and safety
Shining bright for me.

T.W. Cahill, Sr.
4/1/22

I WORSHIP THE LAMB AND HIM ALONE

I bow my knee before His Throne.
His Glory I seek and nothing else,
Not praise nor accolades nor things for self.

His Kingdom only is my heart's desire
May I ever keep it's passion and fire
Lord may I amidst this chaos and shame
Seek to exalt Your Holy name.

There is no other who can heal our land
Not right nor left nor the will of man
You alone are our only hope
No matter our words or who we poke.

Sweet Jesus I bow and cry to Thee
Come save our land from sea to sea
No other name can we trust
It is either You or we will bust
Blood will flow in city streets
The cross will lay at our feet
So Holy Saviour, Spirit Divine
Come and save the nation of mine.

T.W. Cahill, Sr.
7/2/20

INTO THE RISING SUN I LOOK TODAY

With joy and gladness I surely say
Jesus is Lord of heaven and earth
His glory and radiance
Give life and birth
To all around who will fully yield
Their heart to Him their protecting shield.

When the dark ones come in deceiving light
He will put them to an early flight
That no harm should come to those
Who seek
His redeeming grace in times so bleak.

Lifting up their heads who struggle most
He'll hold them high that they may boast
Jesus is Lord of Heaven and Earth.
Deliverance from sin through the second
birth.

As we yield ourselves to Him
The Holy Spirit will cleanse within
From uncleanness and all selfishness
Filling our hearts with His righteousness
That we partakers of His nature may be
Overflowing with love that others may see,

His Passion for all who in darkness live
Light and life to them He would give.

T.W. Cahill, Sr.
1/12/22

IT'S A BEAUTIFUL DAY

Good morning Lord it's a beautiful day
Looking forward to Your awesome presence
along the way
With grace and wisdom from You alone
Received with gladness from Your Throne.

Guiding each step, thought and desire
Filling our hearts with the power of prayer
To live and walk in a darkened world
With the blood-stained banner of Christ
unfurled.

Bringing hope to all around
That light has come without a sound
To set them free from the curse of sin
Cleaning their hearts deep within
That they may walk in holiness
Through the blood of Christ and His
righteousness.

T.W. Cahill, Sr.
2/25/20

KEEPERS OF THE LIGHT

Along the shores of life
Are we faithful to the One
Who shines in the dark of night?

Do we keep our lights
Shining bright and clear
Glowing in the darkness
In fasting and in prayer?

Does our light of grace and love
Reach out to all who need
Saved from storms all around,
To safe and holy ground.

We are the lower lights that shine
Upon the shores of life
The only hope for dying souls
In the dark waters of sin and strife.

T.W. Cahill, Sr.
4/8/22

LET ME RISE ON EAGLE'S WINGS

Far above the storms of life
Let me ride upon the winds
That causes all the strain and strife
High above the darkened clouds
That scare and terrify
Let me rise above the storm
And in Thy presence fly
With joy and gladness in my soul
I give the Victor's cry.

T.W. Cahill, Sr.
7/14/17

LET ME BE JESUS TO SOME SOUL TODAY

Weary and tired along life's way
Who needs Your hand of love and grace
May they see You in my face.

Let my words be those from You
To bring them healing through and through
May they hear from Your Throne
Your loving thoughts in the tone
Of what I say and where I go
Your presence dear Lord, may they know.

T.W. Cahill, Sr.
10/6/21

MOMENTS WITH THE MASTER

Fresh and new today
Are like gentle liquid raindrops
Along life's weary way.

Moments with the Master
Lift the heart in song
With praises for His presence
When things in life go wrong.

Moments with the Master
Are blessings beyond compare
When those all around us
Seem lost and need our care.

Moments with the Master
Can flood your life this day
With songs of joy and gladness
When you bow your heart and pray.

Moments with the Master
You may have today
As you walk with Jesus
Along life's narrow way.

T.W. Cahill, Sr.
3/21/22

MY SOUL, MY LIFE IS LIFTED UP TO THEE

For gladness in this day I see
Healing grace and strength is mine
As I lean on love divine.

All is well within my soul
For His blood has made me whole
Washing, cleansing deep within
From the bane of inward sin.

O the joy of His Holy love
Coming from the Throne above
Filling heart, soul and mind
Leaving no stain of sin behind.

T.W. Cahill, Sr.
3/8/22

IN DARKNESS, SADNESS SO DEEP WITHIN

Our world is lost in rebellious sin
Against the Master, Lord of life
Living in rejection and stubborn strife.

Darkness prevails across the globe
Man has lost his righteous robe
Stained in blood, hate and rags
Bruised, alone in death he sags.

Yet standing near is the light divine
Waiting patiently to untwine
The tangled mess we have made of things
Giving us hope and a song to sing.

T.W. Cahill, Sr.
2/11/22

RELEASING ALL HIS MAJESTY

Against the powers of hell
He the Holy Mighty One
It's darkness will dispel

There is no force can stand against
This glorious King of Kings,
No power on earth or hell
Will stop the awesome movement
That sets all things well.

Yes He who sits upon the Throne
Will soon appear for all to see
And every soul upon the earth
Will bow on bended knee.

T. W. Cahill
1/25/22

RAINBOWS IN THE SKY

A double rainbow in the sky
It's majestic beauty caught my eye
The radiant colors shine so bright
It looks like daytime in the night.

The rainbow is God's promise to man
That a worldwide flood won't happen again
So when I see two rainbows shine
It lifts and encourages this heart of mine.

The storms I face will never bring
A flood into my life
That will destroy my hope in Him
Despite its furry, despite its strife.

But when it passes I will see
The rainbow in my sky
Reminding me of His faithfulness
That He is standing by.

The storm has passed and all is well
He whispers in my ear
I bow my head and praise His name
And shed a joyful tear.

T.W. Cahill, Sr.
6/23/17

THE HEALING TOUCH OF THE MASTER

The healing touch of the Master
Moving through this body of mine
Restoring my lungs to wholeness
By His grace sublime.

The healing touch of the Master
Flowing through each lung
Removing scars from the surface
Making them new and young.

The healing touch of the Master
I see His Hand just now
Keeping His Holy promise
As in His presence I bow.

T.W. Cahill, Sr.
4/8/22

THE NIGHT SHADOWS

The night shadows breaking in the early dawn,
Heaven's angels waiting for the glory of the
Son,
Devils flee in terror at the sight they see,
The crucified Christ arose in victory.

Men prepared for battle against arrays of foes
Trembled in the presence of the Son
as He rose
Victorious over the darkest night
Humanity would ever know.

Then came brave women searching at dawn
For a way to honor Him whose presence
had drawn
Them out of sin into the heavenly light.
Who would move the mighty stone that kept
Him from their sight.

Soon they found the answer clear
He's alive, He's not here
The angel said to those who came
He's gone before you to Galilee
Where His glory you will see.

T.W. Cahill, Sr.
4/22/22

SIXTY-SIX YEARS AND COUNTING

His glory has filled my soul,
He's never left or failed me
But continually has make me whole,
Washing away debris
That sin had left behind.

This marvelous, majestic Saviour
Has been so sweet and kind.
Giving hope and joy
When life was hard and harsh
He put His arms around me
And my tears, away were washed.

Throughout these years,
I've learned to trust my Lord,
His faithful loving kindness;
He has always kept His Word.

As years go by
And age keeps coming on
I'm glad I learned to lean upon
The Father, Spirit and Son.

T.W. Cahill, Sr.
12/31/21

THE MORNING LIGHT GATHERS

The morning light gathers
Upon the rolling fields
The glory of His presence
New life and joy yields.

Surely the fresh new flowers
That spread their pedals out
Bring hope love and peace
That cause the heart to shout.

Another day has dawned
For God to answer prayer
For those who hunger now
Whose hearts are full of care.

Yes, the morning light does gather
Tis awesome for us to see
The Master's heavenly blessing
Our hope of victory.

T.W. Cahill, Sr.
3/16/22

THE WINDOW OF MY SOUL IS OPEN

The window of my soul is open
Looking toward the eastern sky
For my Lord's soon returning
Not someday or by and by.

Events are shaping daily
That seem to tell me now
It won't be long before we see Him
Split the eastern sky.

So keep your heart in tune
With Jesus
Read His Word and daily pray
For signs are showing
He'll soon be on His way.

T.W. Cahill, Sr.
3/16/22

WHAT SHALL I SAY OF MY WONDERFUL LORD

What shall I say of my wonderful Lord
King of Kings and the Living Word
Joy and peace He brings to the soul
By redeeming love He makes us whole.

Hope beyond our wildest dreams
Grace and mercy from His presence streams
Filling each day with gladness and cheer
Knowing each moment He is near.
Whatever may come into our life
His wisdom and power will keep us right,
Victorious over whatever may come
We'll safely reach our heavenly home.

T.W. Cahill, Sr.
4/21/22

WAITING FOR THE MASTER

Waiting for the Master
To flood my soul anew
With glory, grace and victory
That these days seem so few.

My heart must bow anew today
As in His presence I simply wait
For fresh anointing from His Throne
That He can give and He alone.

I open now my weary heart
For that refreshing Lord
Come now; Thy glory impart
Through Thy Living Word.

T.W. Cahill, Sr.
3/18/22

www.ingramcontent.com/pod-product-compliance
Lightning Source LLC
Chambersburg PA
CBHW061317120726
48001CB00002B/556